Through the Eyes Of A Broken Soul

Risha Rozay

Risha Rozay

Through The Eyes Of A Broken Soul

Copyright © 2020 by Marisha Satterwhite

All Rights Reserved.

Reproduction of text in whole or in part without expressed written consent by the author is not permitted and is unlawful according to the 1976 United States Copyright Act.

Printed in the United States of America

Published in the United States by Pen2Pad Ink Publishing.

Requests to publish work from this book or to contact the author should be sent to: ribandz23@gmail.com

Marisha Satterwhite retains the rights to all images

Risha Rozay

Contents

1. All That Glitters Isn't Gold
2. This is Me
3. Love Don't Live Here Anymore
4. Great Sex
5. Unhealed Wounds
6. Dear Heartache and Pain
7. Ecstasy
8. A Long Walk from No Where
9. Cries Are Works of Art
10. The Day You Got Your Wings
11. Sounds Like a Love Song
12. Incestrial Secrets
13. Different
14. An Early Demise
15. Almost Forever
16. Ashes to Ashes & Dust to Dust
17. This Bitch Came For Me

18. His Pleasure Her Pain

19. That's Cute

20. Cease Fire

21. I Lost Myself

22. Starve It

23. In My Father's Absence

24. Love Letter

26. Traveling Through Life

27. Other Books By Risha Rozay

All That Glitters Isn't Gold

See looking at me
you may not know where I come from
or have the slightest idea on where I've been
From depression to rape
to abandonment
I don't even know where I should begin
so let's just start from the beginning
Born to a black queen
Lost in a bad dream
For me was far different than most
My daddy was gone
He left and never came home
The father I once knew was a ghost

He chose crack over me
so he chased his addiction
He disappeared when I needed him most
But my mom was present

Even with her addiction and
battling demons of her own
She still did the best she could
I never went hungry
I always had shelter
But life for me still wasn't good
Take a look at my life
and see what I see
You will see all that glitters isn't gold
On the other side of the grass isn't greener
and some stories are better untold

As I struggled with my own identity
trying to figure out who I wanted to be
Born into the wrong body
Trapped in the wrong life
I didn't want the one given to me
But someone once told me
God gives his toughest battles
to his strongest soldiers
And that I will never forget
Through struggle and strife
I was given this life
because I was strong enough to live it

Through The Eyes of a Broken Soul

When I became a teen
I chose to become a queen
The diva in me wasn't built to be king
many said I was an abomination
and that I had let the devil take hold of me
I started to believe that to be true

When my innocence was stolen from me
You want to be a woman
I'll show you what it feels like to be a woman
Those words sometimes still haunt me
as he ripped away my clothes
Shoving his fingers in my hole
What little joy I had left in me was killed
If you look at my life
and see what I see
You will see all that glitters isn't gold
on the other side the grass isn't greener
and some stories are better untold

Many nights I laid awake contemplating suicide
Drowning in the depths of my sorrow
Soaking in the pool of my tears
no hope for unpromised tomorrow's

A product of my own environment
I thought drugs could somehow ease my pain
And when I realized I couldn't
eat away my sorrow
That's when I turned to cocaine
I laughed to keep from crying
Smiled to hide the hurt
Got high to get by
but that still didn't work

My battle isn't over yet
I will not let depression control me
My story is beginning the rest is unwritten
This test only prepares me for my testimony
So if you look at my life
and see what I see you will see
All that glitters isn't gold
on the other side the grass isn't greener
and some stories are better untold

This is Me...

This is Me
From the switch in my walk
to the softness in my talk
This is me

I don't care who you want me to be
From the hair styles, extensions,
and weaves however, I wear my hair
To the dresses, the skirts, the shoes, or
the tightness in the clothes that I wear
This is me

I don't care who you want me to be
From the lip gloss on my lips
to the curve in my hips
or the distinct thickness of my thighs
This is me

I don't care who you want me to be
From the lumps on my chest
that I love to call breasts
or the eye shadow I wear on my eyes

This is me

I don't care who you want me to be
I guess the point that
I'm trying to make is that this is what makes me
feel happy & free
And whether you accept it or
not this is me
I don't care who you want me to be.

Love Don't Live Here Anymore

I don't know why I believe you
In the back of my mind
I know you lying
I guess I only believed you
when you told me you loved me
Cause in my heart I was tired of crying
See I was searching for a real love
That with the right one
it's like you can't lose
Yet on my journey while searching
it's like I always fall for
those same dudes
You know the gangtas,
the hustlas, the player type,
And no matter how much I love them
I still get played right
Well not today here's a ticket
for your playa flight
I can do bad by myself
You can get on with ya player life

And whatever game you playin'
I hope you play it right
Because you might end up lonely
without a player's wife
Because I refuse to be played
I said I refuse to be played
So, I refuse to let you
play me like an Xbox
Cause when I get hip to all the
bull shit boy the sex stops
Along with everything I do

Meaning I can keep my cash
And you can go back to
po pimping wit cha sorry ass
Cause I don't need a man &
I don't need a spouse
So, you can go back to living in the
basement of ya mamas house
You were the one I loved,
the one I trusted,
the one I would and always
forever adore
But you abandoned me
and love don't live here anymore.

Great Sex

So, we had been sitting by the bar
chilling all night
And the question came out of the blue like
>*He said,*

"What are you doing when the club's over?"
See I had a couple still I was kind of sober
>*He said,*

"Leave with me. Hop in my range rover
but go & tell ya friend."
>*I said,*

"I already told her"
>*He said,*

"So, you had been ready for this"
>*I said,*

"By coincidence ya lips is what I couldn't resist"

I was watching you licking
them and I was hoping you could
be licking me
Then you might take ya tongue out
and deeply put ya dick in me

Start fucking me softly
Slowly bringing out the freak in me
If it was good I might ask you
what you think of me

Do you think its bomb?
Do you think I got a grenade box?
And at the right explosion
I might blow up on ya bomb pop
Like a Popsicle lick you like an icicle
Start sucking you
Throat fucking you till my tonsils tickle
Let me stop
I know I'm sounding kind of freak
But when you deep
Finna skeet
Pull out Nut on my ass cheeks

See it was great sex
The type that make ya leg shake
Cause he was tossing me...
turning me...
flipping me like a pancake
I'm screaming give it to me hard
but slow down before the bed breaks

I had to light a cigarette
He had that have you crawling up the wall dick
Cause he was bending my legs back
Fucking me like I'm a small bitch
I started to make it clap
Now we defining lust
Then I started to throw it back
Until he finally bust
Fuck rated R
I like it rated X
There's no limit to this shit
when you are having great sex

Unhealed Wounds

I keep telling myself that I'm over it
So, I try my best not to care
I keep telling myself that I'm healed
but if I remove these scabs
then my wounds are still there
They are just as fresh as they were before
and they hurt just as bad as they did
But I am the reason my wounds are not healed

So, I guess I deserve what I get
I allowed Him to play me and string me along
and I believed every word
he had spoken
I held on to his lies cause I seen love in His eyes
But in the end my heart was still broken
I hated my mama for her choices in life
And I blamed her for my bad decisions
But I am the weapon, I am the knife,

Through The Eyes of a Broken Soul

I am the cause of my own painful incisions

I resented my father for abandoning me
and his failure in being a man
But I am my own destruction
and for reasons I don't understand
I will never forgive him for what he had done
But I will try my best to forget
He left me with a sorrow so severe
I still haven't learned to cope with
Looking at me you might not know
where I come from

Or have the slightest idea on where I've been
But my story is unique and not told
By many I've been to hell and back again
For my story is unique and
not told from heart aches
and pain to a new beginning?
My wounds are where I will start

The neglect, the rape, the abandonment

and the pain of a broken heart
I can't rewrite my past or undo
what's been done
And I can't change the way that I feel
But to love and to learn to forgive and forget
Is the only way that my wounds will heal.

Dear Heartache & Pain

You have always been there
You have always been a part of me
You were the cause of my depression
You were the IN of my insecurity
You were the ache that lives
inside my heartache

You are the force behind my pain
You were the darkness
in the back of my eyelids
You are the blood that
flows through my veins
You are the point when I wanted
to give up on life
You are the cries inside of my tears
You are the wrists that I
forcefully slit with a knife
You are the monster that

Risha Rozay

resides in my fears

You are my mother that was
addicted to crack cocaine
And loved her pipe more than
she loved her kids
Who gave two fucks about what we did
You are my father who gave up on me
You are my father that was never there
You are the tears in the eyes of my sister

You were my stepfather
that seldomly cared
You were the creep that
tried to rape me
You are his face that
I still see in my dreams
You are the reminder of
how close he came
I can still feel his fingers in me

You are the cousin
that stole my virginity
Before I could make it to high school
You were all the children

that bullied me
You are all the kids
that were ever so cruel
You are the juvenile in jail cells
I sit in for stealing things just to survive

You are the best friend that
I miss so much
And the grandmother
I wish was still alive
You are the funeral of my
hopes and dreams
You are the cremation
of my goals in life

You are the reason
I am mentally, physically
and emotionally
broken and so close to being insane
But I will not let you dictate
my life anymore
So, this is my letter to
heartache and pain

Ecstasy

He whispered in my ear
and asked if I was ready
Before I could answer
He started sucking the bottom of my ear lobe
and kissing my neck
Even if I had planned to say no my body had already said yes.
He lifted my arms above my head
and took off my shirt
all the while still kissing me passionate and slow.

At this point I was ready to receive
everything he had planned for me
He then took one of my succulent titties
into his mouth sucking and
nibbling on my nipple
and then switched to the next
I put my hand inside his grey sweatpants
Anxious to feel his throbbing man hood
Boldly I pulled his pants to his ankles

Through The Eyes of a Broken Soul

and took him into my mouth
slowly sliding every inch of him
to the back of my neck
He moaned in complete pleasure
About 20 mins I performed
Singing to his mic

Then he told me to turn around
and get on my knees up on the couch
He lifted my skirt up around my stomach
I took one leg out of my panties
He then buried his face into the bottom of me
from behind chills quickly crept up my spine
Through muffled moans
I begged him to fuck me
He then slowly entered me from behind
spreading my cheeks as he slid in me
slowly I arched my back
and accepted all of him
Tears began rolling down my cheeks
as I cried moaned and screamed
in total pleasure

He was fuckin so good

Risha Rozay

I felt as though my soul had left my body
In that very moment I begged for it faster
I begged for it harder
I begged him to destroy me
He violently fucked me as
I begged him not to stop
I was yelling God's name
as we both raced to reach our climax
Just as he reached his peak, he pull out of me
and released his heavy load
all over my back and my ass

He was finger fuckin me as he stroked his self
Releasing the rest it still rock hard
He slid back into me
This time stroking me slow
I melted more and more with ever thrust
DAMN
That did it I've made it to ecstasy
I'm coming I screamed at the top of lungs
just before I collapsed
completely drained and over exhausted
Damn we gone have to throw this couch away

A Long Walk From No Where

A long walk from nowhere
lost in the distance
I've been down this road before
But still my mind is in resistance

This sight unknown to my eyes
as if my mind was defaced
And memories in a twist
as if my mind was erased

My body's getting tired...
My legs are getting weak
My thoughts are exhausted...
I'm too tired to think

Don't know where I'm going
All I know is where I've been
I know where I started

Risha Rozay

but who knows where I will end
Suppose I reached my destination
if I ever get there
Yet I came from nothing
a long walk from no where

Cries Are Works of Art

I cried today while painting a picture
And as the tears rolled down my face
drowning my cheeks
Soaking the top of my t-shirt
I thought of you

Wishing my pain stopped
Tears falling like rain drops
And I realized you are
the reason I hurt
And all the while foot prints of my past
tip toe through my mind

Images of you dance behind
my eye lids
I reach for your neck because
I just want to hurt you
the same way you're cheating
and lies did

Risha Rozay

The same way you're cheating
kept me awake at night
The same way your lies made me cry
The same way I question my own insecurities
and for reasons I may never know why

Our song came on the radio today
And I listened to the song
as it played along
Before I knew it,
the words had slipped from my lips
"Share my world don't you leave,
promise I'll be here whenever
you need me near"

I tried not to give you the glory
I tried my best to erase you
from my life
So, what if I was supposed
to share your world
So, what if I was supposed to be
your wife
So, as I lie here in silence
deep in my thoughts

Soaked in the tears of today

Through The Eyes of a Broken Soul

Holding in the pain of yesterday
Distant from the hopes of tomorrow
Lost in the sea of uncertainty
Drowning in the depths of my sorrow

Wishing I might never cry again
And if I never cry again
I wouldn't never cry again
I wouldn't even question my tears
I'll just lay in this bed and think of tears
I once shed

On all the nights, I've cried for you
I cried so long and still
I tried to stay strong
And stay committed still
I tried to do
So, if I never love again
Or if I never trust again

I wouldn't even question my heart
I'll just think of this tearful picture
I painted for you
Called cries are works of art

Risha Rozay

The Day You Got Your Wings

That day I remember like yesterday
That day that moment
your named was called
I remember feeling like all the air
was sucked from my body
I was confused and even appalled
I wanted to be angry at you for leaving
but I know it wasn't your choice

I wanted to hug you, hold you,
kiss you once more
I just wanted to hear your voice
That day I remember like yesterday
That day that moment you got your wings
The day that your heavenly throne
was ready among
Other queens and kings

There are many familiar faces

but there was one that
stuck out in the crowd
They sounded the trumpets
you ran into His arms
And He whispered well done
my child I'm proud

I see your smile inside of the clouds
I hear your voice
in the whistle of the wind
And just like a pot of gold
I can find you where
the rainbow ends and begins
I'll never forget when you were born

And all our memories and things
And I'll never forget when you left
The day that you got your wings.

Risha Rozay

Sounds Like a Love Song

I remember giving when I felt like
I couldn't take it
And I remember how they
doubted me

Told me I wouldn't make it
But all I knew was how to grind
So, I go get it when I wake up
Approaching every proposition
Intentions to get that cake

Remember how I never felt pretty
without the weave and the makeup
And every time I fell in love
I found another reason to break up
Trust issues got my heart cold
Feeling like I'm a target
Self-esteem at its lowest definition
broken hearted

Oh, you waiting for the ending
Well I'm only getting started
Sounds like a love song
But the love has departed

Incestrial Secrets

Family secrets got me
contemplating suicide
Nothing to live for
So, all I wanna do is die
I'd rather give up
than be forced to live another lie
I come and go like the feelings
of my mother's high

I feel unanswered like the
questions in her sister's death
I'm chasing honesty
but lies got me out of breath.
Rapes covered up with the silence
of another wealth

Forced to pack away the pain
Then wonder what causes
my mental health issues
Scared to face the issue

Through The Eyes of a Broken Soul

But the pain behind these tears
can't be dried with a tissue

When you're gone will they miss you
Will they long to hug and kiss you?
Will some be so heartbroken that
they will wanna travel with you?
My final words will be with you

I wish you could have felt what they felt
when he stole their innocence
I wish someone would have
found the courage to stand up
for the innocent
I wish you could have saved her
from physical abuse
I wish you didn't fall victim
to substance abuse

I wish you could have warned him
of the dangers of this world
I wish you never judged him
for becoming a girl
I wish you the best and I pray
these memories will rest as you sleep

Risha Rozay

Along with the lies we tell
And the secrets we keep

Different

Tried to wish it away
That wish ain't come true
Mic check let me give
this beat a run through
When I wanted to escape
who can I run to?
All I wanna do is shine like the sun do

See I'm different from them broads
that was made up
And I'm different because
I never ever gave up
Steady praying to the Lord
Come save us
Because we different
everybody wanna change us

I tried to drink it away
Cause I wanna cry
Tried to smoke it away
It's better when I'm high

Risha Rozay

Truthfully, I could never
tell another lie
Brokenhearted from the tears
in my mother's eyes
Just wanna live
never meant to make my mother cry
What could I give to give it up and
live a different life

An Early Demise

I'm not the way I was and
things are not the way they used to be
I've seen a lot of shit
So I envision shit kinda differently

He stimulated me mentally
Pretended he was into me
He courted me consistently
touched me with such intensity

I think he's the reason why
I don't trust niggas
Why I'm scared to hug and kiss niggas
Why I can never fall in love
with another fuck nigga

So, instead I use them
when I only wanna fuck niggas
When my fund's running low
and my rent due
You can judge but you don't know

Risha Rozay

what I done been through
And you don't care

I really hate when you pretend to
I hold my tongue because
I'm not trying to offend you
If this was you I would
only try to defend you

That's why I fight my battles on my own
Only cry when I'm alone
When I'm hurting they never know
All I wanted was to belong
I just wanted to be accepted
Drowning in my depression
Reminded of his deception
When I think of what I invested

I'm still haunted by his lies
Hurting from his goodbyes
Weeping with weary eyes and
plotting on his demise.

Almost Forever

I wanted forever with you
but forever was wanting too much
I wanted to forever fall weak
to your kiss
I wanted to forever to get lost
in your touch

I wanted forever with you
I wanted forever for us
I wanted forever to love you
wanted forever to lust
I wanted forever but I settled for never
because I forever I never would feel.

We were perfect together just not perfect forever
I'll love you forever still
Visions of forever's
Tomorrow wither my effort to feel,
yesterday in love, today

I love and tomorrow
I'll love you still,
I wanted forever with you

Risha Rozay

I do I did and I will
But forever was so distant
to me forever.

Ashes to Ashes & Dust to Dust

I showered you with affection
I worshipped you with emotion
I covered you in dedication and
I smothered you with devotion

I made excuses for nights
you stayed out late
Trying to hold back tears
that could not wait
Impatient tears form
puddles behind my
restless eyelids, waiting for
you to come home

Ignoring the voice of my conscious,
that kept screaming you were

doing me wrong
Debating with my common sense
that learned
to be ok with you stringing me on
Arguing with my intuition
that kept telling me to leave you alone

My body at war with itself,
my mind said
leave but my feet wouldn't move
My heart stood still as a statue and
waited in hopes you would prove

Prove that you love me like
I wanted to believe
Promise your devotion and
to never deceive
Kiss away my pain with
lying lips that relieve
To have and to hold your heart
was mines to retrieve

Through The Eyes of a Broken Soul

I wanted so desperately
to believe you and
trust in every word had spoke

But your actions spoke
as loud as your lies
And your words resembled a joke
But I couldn't find humor in the
cause of my sorrow
I couldn't just laugh at my pain
I couldn't find hope in
unpromised tomorrows
because yesterday was
too late to explain

So today I surrender to love's
untimely demise
and lay to rest my devotion and trust
Then buried the lies that you told
ashes to ashes and dust to dust

This Bitch Came for Me

How dare you come for me?
You only mad cause he's
Layin' up under me
But I'm unbothered
I go everywhere comfortably

You couldn't see me bitch
Even if you was in front of me
How dare you come for me
If you gone come for me
make sure you come correct
Don't beat around the bush
bitch be very direct
And I hope yo ass can cash it
When yo mouf' write that check

Because I'm the type of bitch
that demands respect
If that's yo nigga my apologies

but I stand correct
this ain't personal it's just business
bitch that bag correct

You came for me without
doin' yo research
how dare you come for me
I don't know where you
received the invitation
but it wasn't from me

I told him to answer when you called
that he ain't gotta stunt for me
And he still hit decline just to show me
that he fucks with me

So the next time you decide
to come for me
or come for a bitch like me
Remember a bitch checkin' me
like Nike is very fuckin unlikely
You would be better off checking
the balance on yo link card
Cuz I'll beat a bitch if they blink hard

Think about it and bitch think hard
Cuz imma go to work with no key card
A lot of bitches might
fold under pressure
but I promise I'm not even
gone bend for you
So, the next time you come for me
just make sure I send for you.

His Pleasure Her Pain

HE RAPED ME!
Ain't nobody fuckin raped you
There you go makin' up lies again
That's the exact reason why
I bottle emotions and my
pain lies within,

Because you're always so quick
to second guess me
Why must I pretend
Like I'm not a victim,
like I haven't been hurt,
ain't nobody gotta lie on your friend

Look I'm not having conversation with you.
You'll say anything to keep me
from being happy,
No that's where you're wrong
that dick got you blind

Risha Rozay

yea I said it and I don't care
if you slap me,

You were supposed to protect me
instead you neglected me
because you don't wanna be alone,
I'm not having this
conversation with you
I wish you would leave me alone,
No, I'm not gonna leave you alone
he didn't leave me alone
and you left me alone with him,

When you're at work
I'm at home with him,
He can go to hell for what he did to me
and you can go with him,

I sleep fully clothed because
I don't wanna make it easy for him,
Then you pick up extra shifts at work
and you make it easy for him,
Don't cry now I'm lyin' remember
I know you seen the blood
on my sheets

Through The Eyes of a Broken Soul

when you washed,
If you wasn't gon' do nothin'
or even say something you
might as well stood there and watched

Go to your room
We're not having this conversation
I hate you
You're pathetic and weak
That night I cried myself to sleep
Wanting to give up on life as I weep,

When he got home from work that night
she shot a bullet through his brain
I guess she believed me after all
She didn't even give
him a chance explain
She was a victim herself
when she looked
in my eyes she saw her own pain
So she knew she had to do something
and end his pleasure her pain

That's Cute

The dumbest shit I ever heard was
you cute to be a big girl
As if size had a weight limit
If pretty means small, medium or large
I'm sorry I can't fit it
A lot of niggas like big girls
so fuck who ain't wit it

If you're not licensed to
handle heavy equipment
I'm sorry you can't get it
Is my beauty really defined
by my hips and my thighs
Because they're larger than most
I'm not qualified to be fine
Because my stomach is big
and my bottom is wide
Sorry to misinform
whoever told you that lied

Through The Eyes of a Broken Soul

The beauty I know comes in
different shapes and sizes
And the beauty I own is confident
no man can deprive it
The beauty I see in the faces of friends

Comes in extra, extra larges
beauty hasn't always been thin
Beauty is something that lies within
And sayin' things like that to women
is why self-esteem issues hides within
So, load your words carefully
the next time you shoot
Because I'm not cute to be big girl
Bitch I'm cute to be cute

Cease Fire

In my city all I see is death,
surrounded by pain,
man my city need help,
Why the murder?
Why beef?
Why we killin' each other?
Why can't we kick it without shooting
and running for cover?

It ain't safe in the streets of rock
ever other day it's like a nigga get shot
Body's start droppin'
when the weather gets hot
9-11-16 my lil cousin got shot
rest in peace Phe
When they took you
man I swear they took of piece of me

We want more but what is more?
What is it really like?
More of the murders the killings

and the candle lights
Grippin' the handle on the gun
but can you handle life

Behind bars locked down
you hearing me right,
But are you listening?
We so broken but it's time to fix it
It could be you or someone you
love that becomes another statistic
We want more but what is more?
What is it really like?

Parents play ya position
Prepare your children for jobs and
entrepreneurial positions
Pay for college tuition
Save yo sons from these guns or rottin' in prison
We want more but what is more,
what is it really like

Less disease, more degrees
and succeeding in life
I came from the valley
the shadow of death
but since they killed my cousin

Risha Rozay

on her way home
I stay to myself
I'm so for real
It's really real up in the field
From Spring Creek to Springfield
you can get killed
We want more, safer streets
I can't wait till it ends
Let's come together and
make our city great again!

I Lost Myself

I lost myself, and I've been
lookin' all over
but I can't seem to figure out
where I left me
I've searched near and far,
high and low
but I just can't seem to figure out
where I might be

I thought I'd find me in the
bottom of a bottle
or maybe in the duck of a blunt
I thought maybe I was lost in a line
so, looked for me in the
bottom of a bag

I remember when I was down
at my lowest
but I knew I didn't leave me there
but if I wasn't low then I had to be high so,

Risha Rozay

I went chasing a high, thinking maybe
I might find me there

I almost ran out of gas on my journey to high so,
I popped pills to refuel my tank
and once I got there,
I still didn't find me
Damn where did I lose myself?

I looked for me in the arms of a man,
in the arms of many men
but none of them could
help me find me
none of them even knew who I was

They told me they could
help me find me
and that they would lead me
back to myself
but still I ended up with nothing
I wonder where the hell I might be

I looked for me at my mother's
thinking maybe I had left me there
but my mother said she hadn't seen me

Through The Eyes of a Broken Soul

she was on her way to high so,
I figured maybe she lost herself too

I told her I had just came from
there lookin' for me and I didn't see her there
when I left she said that was the last place she
had been so, she decided to go check herself

I looked for me in the
bottom of a pill bottle
thinkin' maybe I'd find me in my dreams
but when I woke up in a hospital stomach
turning, vomiting up a black liquid
that tasted of charcoal

I knew I wouldn't find me there
I looked for me in the absence of my father
In the hatred of my rapist
In the regret of my ex's
In the mistakes of my past
In the love of my sister

I even looked for me
at the altar of a church
but the hypocrites told me

Risha Rozay

I hadn't been there
I lost myself and
I've been lookin' all over,
but I just don't know where I could be
I lost myself and I'm still trying to find me
Was I here?
Have you seen me?

Starve It

Anything that you don't want
to live in your life starve it.
If you don't feed it, it won't grow.
Don't feed addiction
don't feed depression
don't feed into negativity
don't feed temptation
don't feed sadness
don't feed hurt
don't feed pain
don't feed distraction

You are on an assignment and
you will not be moved
Tell the devil,
I'm sorry but you can't eat here
no more
Depression has been real
but this kitchen is closed
Addiction it was fun while it lasted

but we are no longer open for service
We are under construction
this restaurant is closed indefinitely
Temptation I'm sorry I can't serve you
we've redone our menu
We no longer serve anything you eat
try the McDonald's down the street
sadness, hurt, pain

I understand that you all want your
usual table for three
but I'm sorry we're hosting
a private party
for joy and happiness
you can't eat here tonight
we do apologize for the inconvenience

Distraction yes, I'm cooking for Thanksgiving
but I'm sorry you can't come
I will not feed you
you are not invited
you've stood in my way long enough
you have crippled my growth and
held me back far too long
could you move please

Anything that has set out
to destroy you starve it.
Whatever that has set forth
to stand in your way
don't feed it
If its hungry enough it will move
If you don't feed it, it won't grow

In My Fathers Absence

It takes a real man to raise a child
he didn't make
But in my father's absence he stood filling
the footprints of someone else's mistake
To love and care for that child with each day that it wakes
He would parent that child for as long as it takes

In my father's absence he stood
Loving me no different than those of his flesh
He raised me the best way he could
In my father's absence he taught me what my real father should
In my father's absence he cared for me
He was always there for me
In my father's absence he punished me when I was wrong
But its also because of him that I am so strong

Through The Eyes of a Broken Soul

It took me almost losing him to realize exactly what he means to me

Because from two until now and the rest our days

he will always be a father to me

He ruled with authority and taught by the belt

I was sure to know right from wrong

In my father's absence he showed me that my father was there all along

Love Letter

But I'll leave you with this,
rest knowing that there's no one in this
world that loves you more than me.
And wherever life takes us,
your heart is always where mine will be.
you will always hold the key to my heart
and deed to my soul
Patiently I wait for the day finally our
lives become whole.
Our paths reunite and our hearts reconnect
Only till then, I can only reflect
replaying our memories and rereading our past
all the while hoping that night
wasn't our last
Just to join a union in life,
And grow old and grey
to have lived and have loved
Would more than be great

With you as my other
I'll stand in your shadow
And forever I'll walk at your side
Wherever life takes us
As long as you drive forever,
I'm down for the ride

Risha Rozay

Traveling Through Life

Your call has been forwarded

to an automatic voice messaging system

Please leave a message after the beep - beeeppp
Father forgive me

because I know that this was not a part of the
path that you had chosen for me,
It's just that somewhere along my journey I got
lost along the way
And ever since I made that wrong turn down
temptations road
I've been desperately trying

to find my way back home

Father I can still feel your presence

walking with me

Even when I'm lost I know you are there

You're with me in the midst of my mess
You said in your word you would never leave
me nor forsake me
And I've always known this to be true
Ashamed to kneel at your feet

because I am not worthy of your grace

Still I call on you

As I've done so many times before
You'll never know God is all you need

until he's all you got
Your all I got father

I have no one else I can call

Can you help me please?

To send your message now press pound
To rerecord your message press star

If you are finished hang up
I'm snapping back
There will be a brief silence while the subscriber
you are trying to reach is being located

Your call was accepted say hi

Hello father are you there?

I know you hear me

You always do,

I humbly come before you

Father I am lost on this road called temptation

I don't know where I'm at or where I'm headed
I never meant to let you down
I know...

I know you told me to take life's pathway

Risha Rozay

It was a straight shot
That it would lead me all the way there
and it was not going to be an easy ride
but at some point, about half way there
I came to a fork in the road
and my GPS signal was lost
and I...I

That's when you should have called me
a voice spoke unto me,
don't wait till (midnight)
don't just call at your darkest hour
You'll never know God is all you need
until he's all you got
Never forget that I'm on my way
Your call has been disconnected goodbye

Aspire to Inspire Before You Expire!!!

Other Books by Risha Rozay

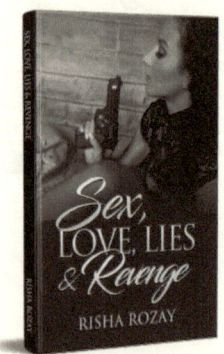

Get connected with *Author Risha Rozay* on social media

 Author Risha Rozay

 risharozay

Through The Eyes of a Broken Soul

www.ingramcontent.com/pod-product-compliance
Lightning Source LLC
Chambersburg PA
CBHW060411080526
44583CB00012B/531